JOHNNY SAIN

GREG MADDUX

EDDIE MATHEWS

DALE MURPHY

CHARLES NICHOLS

HANK AARON

CHIPPER JONES

GEORGE SISLER

ANDRUW JONES

RED SCHOENDIENST

TOM GLAVINE

WARREN SPAHN

THE HISTORY OF THE
ATLANTA
BRAVES

WAYNE STEWART

CREATIVE 🍎 EDUCATION

Published by Creative Education, 123 South Broad Street, Mankato, MN 56001

Creative Education is an imprint of The Creative Company.

Designed by Rita Marshall.

Photographs by AllSport (Al Bello, Scott Cunningham, Doug Pensinger), Associated Press/Wide World

Photos, FotoSport (Mitch Reibel), Icon Sports Media (David Seelig), National Baseball Library,

SportsChrome (Jonathan Kirn, Rob Tringali Jr.)

Library of Congress Cataloging-in-Publication Data

Stewart, Wayne, 1951- The history of the Atlanta Braves / by Wayne Stewart.

p. cm. — (Baseball)   ISBN 1-58341-200-X

Summary: Highlights the key personalities and memorable games in the history of the team that

moved to Atlanta from Milwaukee in 1966.

1. Atlanta Braves (Baseball team)—History—

Juvenile literature. [1. Atlanta Braves (Baseball team)—History.

2. Baseball—History.] I. Title. II. Baseball (Mankato, Minn.).

GV875.A8 S84 2002   796.357′64′09758231—dc21   2001047858

First Edition 9 8 7 6 5 4 3 2 1

JUST BELOW

THE APPALACHIAN MOUNTAINS, ROOTED FIRMLY IN THE

deep South, is the city of Atlanta, Georgia. Once surrounded by

majestic plantations and sprawling countryside, the city is today

known for its rapid urban expansion. Life in Atlanta was once

genteel and relaxed, but the city now pulsates with the energy of

many major corporations, including the Coca-Cola Company.

Atlanta is also home to a professional baseball team called the

Braves, which traces its roots to Boston. The Braves began playing in

Boston during the early 1870s and joined the National League (NL)

for its inaugural season in 1876. In 1953, the team moved to

Milwaukee before finally settling in Atlanta in 1966. Since moving

south, the Braves have become as much a part of the city's summers

HUGH DUFFY

as the area's plentiful peach trees and busy boulevards.

{THE MODERN ERA BEGINS} The Braves were a strong

In their early years, the Braves were also some- times called the Doves, Beaneaters, or Red Caps.

team in their early years thanks to such players as hard-hitting outfielder Hugh Duffy. In 1890, Boston became even more powerful with the addition of star pitcher Charles "Kid" Nichols. Nichols won 27 games as a rookie in 1890 and went on to win at least

6 30 games in seven other seasons. Behind Nichols and curveball

expert Vic Willis, Boston won five NL pennants in the 1890s.

By 1905, however, both Nichols and Willis were gone, and the

Braves plummeted, losing 100 or more games in six seasons from

1905 to 1912. After the 1912 season, Boston brought in new manager

George Stallings. "I've been stuck with some terrible teams in my

day," muttered Stallings of his 1913 crew, which again finished deep

in the standings, "but this one beats them all."

TOM GLAVINE

Charles "Kid" Nichols starred on the mound but also played the outfield and first base.

CHARLES NICHOLS

The 1914 season was a different story, though. That year, the

Braves performed a miracle by soaring to the NL pennant with

94 victories—a one-year improvement of 25 wins.

More incredibly, Boston remained in last place at

midseason before suddenly getting hot and winning 52

of its last 66 games.

Even though they featured only one truly great

hitter—outfielder Joe Connolly—the Braves won the pennant by

10½ games, thanks in large part to the efforts of pitchers Bill James

and Dick Rudolph. Then, in the World Series, catcher Hank Gowdy

hit .545, and Boston's pitching overwhelmed the Philadelphia

Athletics as the Braves won the world championship in a four-game

sweep. Incredibly, the Braves had gone from doormats to champs in

one year, and newspapers called the Braves' 1914 season "the greatest

comeback story in baseball annals."

Second baseman Johnny Evers slapped 20 doubles in **1914** and captured the NL MVP award.

JOHNNY EVERS

A **1990s** standout, Ryan Klesko was equally skilled in the outfield or at first base.

RYAN KLESKO

{THE NOT-SO-ROARIN' '20s AND '30s} For quite some time after 1914, Boston experienced one losing season after another.

In **1921**, slow-footed catcher Ernie Lombardi batted .330— still a club record for catchers.

Fortunately, fans were able to root for a number of outstanding Braves players. Two stars of the early 1920s were infielders Rabbit Maranville and Dave "Beauty" Bancroft. The 5-foot-5 Maranville was a valuable clutch hitter, while Bancroft was known for his great range and sure glove at shortstop. Bancroft was also known for his talkative nature and earned his nickname by shouting "Beauty" after every good pitch to opposing batters.

Two other Hall-of-Famers also spent time with the Braves during that era: Rogers Hornsby and George Sisler. Hornsby, a second baseman, played just one season in Boston (1928) but carved his name into the team's record books with a .387 average and the NL batting title. Many baseball experts still consider Hornsby the

RABBIT MARANVILLE

greatest right-handed hitter of all time.

Sisler, meanwhile, was a graceful first baseman who could hit

the ball a mile. The lean lefty twice batted above .400 and was also

an agile fielder. "He's the nearest thing to a perfect ballplayer," said

legendary Detroit Tigers outfielder Ty Cobb. "He can do everything—

hit, hit with power, field, run, and throw."

Outfielder Wally Berger emerged as another Boston star in the 1930s. In his first season (1930), he smacked 38 home runs, an

Six Braves players appeared in the **1948** All-Star Game, including ace hurler Johnny Sain.

NL rookie record. Yet despite his best efforts and those of Boston's other stars, the Braves remained a mediocre team. From 1917 to 1946, Boston never finished higher than fourth place in the NL standings.

{ANOTHER PENNANT AT LAST} In 1947, Boston

showed signs of life, leaping to third place. A year later, the Braves finally captured another NL pennant, going 91–62 under manager Billy Southworth. One phrase summed up Boston's success that season: "Spahn and Sain, then pray for rain." Translated, that meant that the Braves' pitching staff basically revolved around just two players—Warren Spahn and Johnny Sain.

Sain won a league-best 24 games in 1948, while Spahn added 15. Eventually, though, Spahn established himself as the team's top ace.

DAVID JUSTICE

In 21 seasons, the left-hander topped the 20-win mark 13 times.

Spahn worked with a big windup and an exaggerated high leg kick

before delivering a nasty array of pitches. "I never throw a ball down

the middle of the plate," Spahn said. "In fact, I ignore the 12 inches

in the middle and concentrate on hitting the two and a half inches

on each side or corner of it."

Supplying the Braves' offensive power in 1948 were such great

hitters as rookie shortstop Al Dark, third baseman Bob Elliot, and

outfielder Tommy Holmes. With so much talent, the

Braves were heartbroken when they lost the 1948

World Series to the Cleveland Indians. Sain out-

dueled Cleveland ace Bob Feller 1–0 in the series

opener, but the powerful Indians roared back to win

the championship in six games.

Tommy Holmes (right) became the fifth Braves player to lead the NL in hits (in **1945** and **1947**).

{THE FABULOUS '50s} The Braves moved to Milwaukee,

Wisconsin, in 1953. In their first eight seasons there, the Braves

remained an NL powerhouse. They won pennants in 1957 and 1958

and came close in 1959, finishing in a tie for first before losing the

pennant to the Los Angeles Dodgers in a special playoff series.

The Braves' roster during those years was packed with

superstars, including the durable Spahn and third baseman

TOMMY HOLMES

Catcher Javy Lopez followed in the footsteps of Phil Masi, a star backstop in the '**40s**.

Eddie Mathews, the only man to play for the Braves in Boston, Milwaukee, and Atlanta. Mathews was one of the greatest sluggers

In **1957**, legendary slugger Hank Aaron drove in a career-high 132 runs and was named the NL MVP.

of all time, eventually joining baseball's exclusive 500 home run club and earning a place in the Hall of Fame.

But the greatest Braves player of all was outfielder Hank Aaron. Aaron had huge wrists that enabled him to whip the bat around with great speed, even when

he was a scrawny rookie. From 1954 to 1974, he was the heart of the Braves' offense. Before the end of his career, Aaron set a major-league record with 2,297 RBI and played in 24 All-Star Games.

Aaron's greatest claim to fame, however, was his home run power. He eventually slammed 755 career homers, surpassing Babe Ruth to become baseball's all-time home run king. As Aaron approached Ruth's coveted record, pitchers threw to him very cautiously. "I don't see pitches down the middle anymore—not even

HANK AARON

in batting practice," the outfielder joked.

While Aaron obliterated the ball at the plate, future Hall-of-

Famer Red Schoendienst provided top-notch defense with his great

range at second base. Schoendienst had "the greatest pair of hands

I've ever seen," marveled legendary St. Louis Cardinals outfielder

Stan Musial.

In 1957, Spahn won 21 games, and Lew Burdette won 17. The Braves powered their way to the World Series that year, then beat

the mighty New York Yankees. Burdette was simply spectacular, winning three games in the series with a 0.67 ERA. The next season, Milwaukee returned to the World Series but lost to the Yankees.

{ANOTHER LONG DROUGHT} From 1960 to

1982, the Braves suffered another long dry spell. The only oasis in their desert of losing came in 1969. That season, the Braves (who had moved to Atlanta in 1966) won their first NL Western Division title, only to be knocked off by the New York Mets in the NL Championship Series (NLCS).

Still, Atlanta featured several brilliant players during those decades. Catcher Joe Torre, who would later become a successful big-league manager, represented the Braves in the All-Star Game for

JOE TORRE

The great Warren Spahn led the league in wins eight times from the **1940s** to the **'60s**.

WARREN SPAHN

five straight seasons in the mid-1960s. Over that stretch, he averaged

27 home runs per season. Also starring at the plate were first

baseman Orlando Cepeda and outfielder Rico Carty.

Carty missed the 1968 season battling tuberculosis but

came back to hit .342 and .366 the next two seasons

and win the 1970 NL batting crown.

Pitcher Phil Niekro, meanwhile, was the team's

ace during that period. He used a dancing knuckleball to baffle hitters

and was instrumental during Atlanta's division-winning 1969 season.

Another knuckleball specialist, Los Angeles Dodgers pitcher Tom

Candiotti, once had the opportunity to ask Niekro for pitching

advice when they both played for the Cleveland Indians. "It was like

talking to Thomas Edison about light bulbs," Candiotti recalled.

After 1969, Atlanta plunged back into a losing spiral. In 1976,

wealthy businessman and television mogul Ted Turner bought the

Phil Niekro's fluttering knuckleball earned him 23 wins during Atlanta's surprising **1969** season.

PHIL NIEKRO

Braves franchise, and over the next four seasons, his team finished

dead last. Still, Turner managed to stay upbeat about his team.

"Look at it this way," he quipped. "We're making a lot of people

happy in other cities."

{A DYNASTY BEGINS} In 1982, the Braves at last made

Atlanta fans happy, returning to the playoffs after opening the season 13–0. Leading the way was outfielder Dale Murphy, a team

leader who was named NL Most Valuable Player (MVP) that season

and the next. From 1982 through 1987, Murphy was

sensational, averaging 36 homers and 105 RBI per

season. Although Atlanta lost in the NLCS in 1982

and then slipped back down the standings, a dynasty

was just around the corner.

Longtime star Dale Murphy spent 15 seasons in Atlanta, slamming a total of 371 home runs.

The Braves became a powerhouse in the 1990s under new

manager Bobby Cox. As is the case with most baseball dynasties,

Atlanta's success revolved around great pitching, and no Braves

pitcher was better than Greg Maddux, who captured an

unprecedented four consecutive Cy Young Awards (from 1992 to

1995) as the NL's top pitcher.

Not an overpowering thrower, Maddux—who looked more like

a scholar than an athlete—relied on pinpoint control. He was also an

DALE MURPHY

outstanding defensive player, winning the Gold Glove award every season from 1990 to 2001. "Maddux just never gives you anything to hit," said San Diego Padres outfielder Tony Gwynn. "He just keeps changing speeds and painting the corners. It makes for a long day."

First baseman Fred McGriff batted a team-high .318 during the strike- shortened **1994** season.

Filling out the Braves' fearsome pitching staff were Tom Glavine and John Smoltz. The crafty Glavine earned Cy Young Awards in 1991 and 1998, and Smoltz—a pitcher who couldn't muster a career winning record in the minors—won the award in 1996 with a 24–8 record. "Glavine picks you apart one day, and the next, Smoltz knocks the bat out of your hands," said San Francisco Giants slugger Barry Bonds.

From 1991 to 2001, the Braves won their division every season but one and captured five NL pennants. The main stars on offense were outfielder David Justice and third baseman Chipper Jones.

FRED McGRIFF

In 1991, Justice helped Atlanta make history when it became the

first team ever to reach the World Series just one year after having

baseball's worst record. Justice also starred in 1995,

when Atlanta won its first World Series in 38 seasons.

The left-handed slugger's home run in the final game

of the series won a dramatic 1–0 contest.

A year later, Jones played a big role in guiding

Pitcher John Smoltz ended the **1996** season as the NL's strikeout king, fanning 276 batters.

Atlanta back to the World Series, the team's fourth trip there in five   **29**

postseasons. Although the Braves came up short that year, Jones

continued to excel, winning the 1999 NL MVP award after slamming

45 home runs—a new league record for switch-hitters.

Atlanta continued loading up for the new millennium by adding

such young players as center fielder Andruw Jones in the late

1990s. Jones quickly established himself as one of the game's best

defensive outfielders, covering surprising ground with his speed

JOHN SMOLTZ

A switch-hitter, young short-stop Rafael Furcal was known for his amazing quickness.

RAFAEL FURCAL

Perennial Gold Glove winner Andruw Jones drove in 104 runs in **2000** and again in **2001**.

ANDRUW JONES

and making one highlight catch after another. Atlanta fans counted

on Jones and fellow outfielder Gary Sheffield—who joined Atlanta

in 2002—to keep the Braves riding high for many

years to come.

Over their long history, the Braves have established

themselves as one of baseball's greatest success stories.

In fact, Atlanta is the only major-league team ever to

win 10 consecutive division titles or appear in eight straight league

championship series. As the Braves attempt to keep their dynasty

alive, they will surely continue to heat up the already-warm

summers in Atlanta.

JASON MARQUIS